Little Hymns™

Little Hymns • Silent Night
Written and illustrated by Andy Holmes
Watercolor by Cameron Thorp and Matt Taylor
Music transcription by Marty Franks

Copyright ©1992 by HSH Educational Media Company
P.O. Box 167187, Irving, Texas 75016

First Printing 1992
ISBN 0-929216-50-4
Printed in the United States of America

Published by

PRESS

Little Hymns™

by Andy Holmes

Silent Night

Si - lent night, ho - ly night, all is calm, all is bright

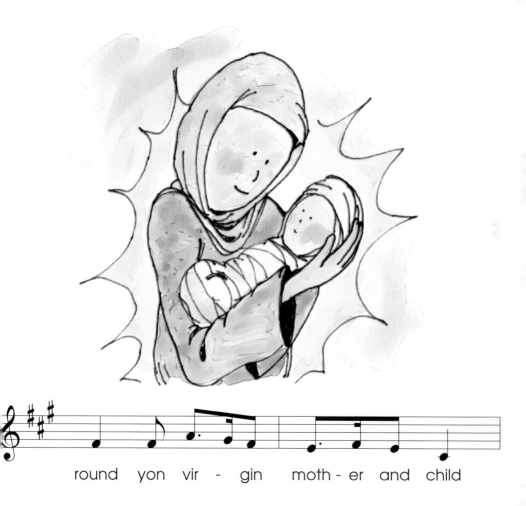

round yon vir - gin moth - er and child

Ho - ly in - fant, so ten - der and mild,

sleep   in   heav - en - ly   peace,

sleep   in   heav - en - ly   peace.

Si - lent night, ho - ly night,

dark - ness   flies,   all   is   light,

shep - herd's hear the an - gels sing,

al - le - lu - ia   to   the   King.

Christ the Sav-ior is born, Christ the Sav-ior is born!

Si - lent night, ho - ly night,

Son of God, love's pure light,

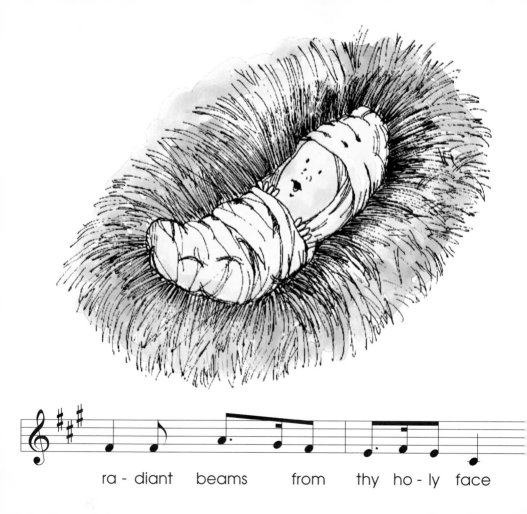

ra - diant   beams   from   thy ho - ly   face

with the dawn of re - deem - ing grace,

Je-sus, Lord, at thy birth,   Je - sus, Lord, at thy birth.

Si - lent night, ho - ly night,

won - drous   star,   lend   thy   light,

with the an - gels let us sing,

al - le - lu - ia   to   our   King.

Christ the Sav-ior is born, Christ the Sav-ior is born!

Silent Night

Si - lent night, ho - ly night, all is calm, all is bright
Si - lent night, ho - ly night, dark - ness flies, all is light,
Si - lent night, ho - ly night, Son of God, love's pure light,
Si - lent night, ho - ly night, won - drous star, lend thy light,

round yon vir - gin moth-er andchild Ho - ly in-fant,so ten - der and mild
shep-herd's hear the an - gels sing, al - le - lu - ia to the King
ra - diant beams from thy ho-ly face with the dawn of re - deem - ing grace
with the an - gels let us sing, al - le - lu - ia to our King

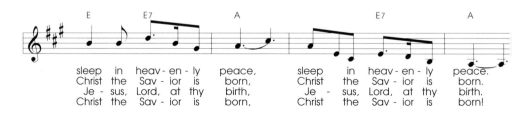

sleep in heav - en - ly peace, sleep in heav - en - ly peace.
Christ the Sav - ior is born, Christ the Sav - ior is born.
Je - sus, Lord, at thy birth, Je - sus, Lord, at thy birth.
Christ the Sav - ior is born, Christ the Sav - ior is born!